NEWCASTLE UNITED

THIRD EDITION

This edition published in 2012
First published by Carlton Books in 2003

This book is not an officially licensed product of
Newcastle United Football Club

Text and design copyright © Carlton Books Limited 2003, 2007, 2012

A CIP catalogue record for this book is available
from the British Library.

ISBN 978-1-84732-940-0

Printed in China

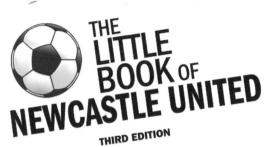

THE LITTLE BOOK OF NEWCASTLE UNITED

THIRD EDITION

Edited by **MIKE BOLAM**

CARLTON
BOOKS

INTRODUCTION

There is no other club like this.

For a century Newcastle have found new ways to amaze, frustrate, delight and exasperate their supporters.

This book attempts the impossible task of conveying that history via a collection of quotes, both from the greats and from those best forgotten.

But in the end there's only really one, universally acknowledged, quote about this club that needs to be recorded:

'Howay the Lads'

66 It was agreed that the club's colours should be changed from red shirts and white knickers to black-and-white shirts (two-inch stripe) and dark knickers. **99**

Minutes of club meeting, 2.8.1894

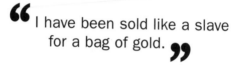

“ I have been sold like a slave for a bag of gold. **”**

Hughie Gallacher *reacts badly to being transferred to Chelsea, 1930*

"Hughie of the Magic Feet is Dead"

*Headline in the **Newcastle Journal**, 12.6.57,*
following the suicide of Hughie Gallacher

66 We're very happy to have won the Cup. Every man in Newcastle has done his duty. **99**

*Captain **Jimmy Nelson**, collecting the FA Cup after the 1932 final*

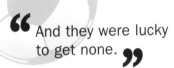

66 And they were lucky to get none. **99**

Len Shackleton *after the 13-0 defeat of Newport County, 5.10.46*

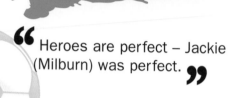

66 Heroes are perfect – Jackie
(Milburn) was perfect. 99

Bobby Charlton

" Jackie Milburn was a fine player – he was quick, he was fast, he had a change of pace, he could play outside-right or centre-forward. **"**

Stanley Matthews *paying tribute to a former England colleague*

66 I was worried to death that no one would turn up. Ten years is a long time. People forget. 99

Jackie Milburn *on his 1967 testimonial.*
Nearly 46,000 attended

" This is the only club I'd come back to just to sweep the terraces. "

Jim Iley, *Magpies stalwart of the 1960s*

66 I regard this as a system from the Middle Ages. It is really treating men like cattle and really the position is that they are paid slaves. **99**

Lord Justice Wilberforce *upholds the legal case brought by Newcastle player George Eastham against the maximum wage, June 1963*

" Too busy walking Charlie Mitten's greyhounds... "

George Graham *explains why he never made the grade as an apprentice at Newcastle*

" He was never a tactical genius but he did a marvellous job of managing Newcastle United. **"**

Frank Clark *on Joe Harvey*

" All you've got to do is score a goal. These foreigners are all the same, they'll collapse like a pack of cards – they've no gumption. **"**

Joe Harvey's *inspirational half-time team talk in the Fairs Cup final second leg, 1969*

" We were a team in the best sense of the word. There were no superstars. No world-beaters, just a damned good team. **"**

Jimmy Scott, *who played all 12 games in the Fairs Cup-winning run of 1968–69, and scored the club's first-ever goal in European competition*

❝ I felt that I understood then what Tyneside was all about – it needed somebody to stick the ball in the net. **❞**

Malcolm Macdonald *reflecting on his home debut hat-trick against Liverpool, 21.8.71*

" Radford – now Tudor's gone down for Newcastle... Radford again, oh what a goal, what a goal! **"**

John Motson *launches his career as a football commentator by describing Hereford's equaliser in the FA Cup, February 1972*

" ... Tudor got it away to Hibbitt... Macdonald is on ahead... what a ball there by Hibbitt and away goes Macdonald again... and that's a magnificent goal! That is number two and that is the killer goal! **"**

*The late **Brian Moore** describes Newcastle's second goal against Burnley in the 1974 FA Cup semi-final*

> **66** May 4, 1974, will haunt me for ever. I feel sick and embarrassed. **99**

Joe Harvey *speaking about the 1974 FA Cup Final humiliation versus Liverpool*

" I remember crouching down and crying at the end of the game and Bill Shankly came across and he put his arm around me and said, "Dinnae worry, son, you'll get there one day." **"**

Malcolm Macdonald *remembers the 1974 FA Cup Final*

" As the manager I have a duty to give them sweat, to give them blood and, to be quite honest, I would die for the club that I worked for. **"**

Gordon Lee *pledges his life to United, literally*

" If I've done it wrong, I'm sorry but I think I did it right and time will show that I did it right. **"**

*An unrepentant **Jack Charlton** interviewed after his resignation as manager*

> **Not a very nice river. Some days you didn't need a bridge to walk across it.**

*Dunston-born **'Rocky' Hudson** muses on the 'coaly' River Tyne*

" Of all 22 I was the only player born within the City walls and north of the Tyne. These lads from Durham and Chester-le-Street don't count. **"**

*Boyhood Toon fan **Denis Tueart** after scoring the winner for Manchester City in the 1976 League Cup Final*

❝ If we as a club – or Bill McGarry as an individual – had wanted a black-and-white army we would have introduced conscription. **❞**

Club programme *editorial after crowd trouble at Hillsborough, 1980*

" It was the saddest day of my life: he was my very best buy. I could watch him play all day and every day. **"**

Joe Harvey *on the day knee ligament trouble forced midfielder Tony Green to quit, December 1973*

66 Craggs forward, Keegan's flick, Varadi, Keegan again – chance here for Keegan... he's done it! Kevin Keegan scores and St James' Park goes absolutely wild! **99**

Commentator **Roger Tames,** *describing Keegan's debut goal against QPR in 1982*

66 I queued for five hours at the Gallowgate end to watch Keegan's first match. **99**

Alan Shearer, *Newcastle fan*

" The crowd sucked it in. **"**

Kevin Keegan *claims a communal assist for his debut goal v QPR*

" In Liverpool you get it from The Kop, but at St James' Park it comes from everywhere. It's like stereo with four speakers! **"**

Kevin Keegan *compares crowd noise at two of his favourite clubs*

66 Surely Bobby Robson could have phoned me. After being involved in the international set-up for ten years, surely I'm worth a ten pence phone call. **99**

Kevin Keegan *on the abrupt curtailment of his England career*

66 The chant from the crowd, if you can follow the Geordie accents, appears to be, "Bobby Robson, are you watching on the box?" **99**

*Commentator **Tony Gubba** as Keegan scored four at Rotherham after being dropped by England manager Robson*

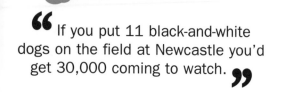

66 If you put 11 black-and-white dogs on the field at Newcastle you'd get 30,000 coming to watch. **99**

Sir Matt Busby

66 If Newcastle win promotion, forget about making Kevin Keegan Player of the Year – he'll deserve to be named Team of the Year. They should rename Newcastle, Keegan United. **99**

Bob Paisley, *Liverpool boss, November 1983*

" Our prices are half Newcastle's prices – you just can't compare the clubs, they're not to compare. We're stuck between a massive city that's vibrant like Newcastle… and Middlesbrough. **"**

*Sunderland chairman **Bobby Murray** and his envy of Tyneside, 2002*

66 I wish we had supporters like Newcastle's. Their supporters are more loyal than ours. One has to be fair – if we'd signed Kevin Keegan, I don't believe we would have had the same reaction through the turnstiles. 99

*Sunderland chairman **Tom Cowie** and his envy of Tyneside, 1982*

❝ I took him off because he wasn't hungry enough for his hat-trick. **❞**

*Hardman **Arthur Cox** explains why he substituted two-goal Chris Waddle, 1983*

" Good evening, Newcastle! **"**

David Bowie *greets the crowd from the stage of...*
Roker Park, Glass Spider Tour, 23.6.87

66 So Brighton kick off this historic match and, as you sample the quite unique atmosphere here at St James' Park, you wonder how British football let alone Newcastle United will ever replace Kevin Keegan. 99

*Commentator **Alan Parry**, 1984*

66 Whatever I've given Tyneside, it's given me a hundred times as much. I hope I'm always their friend and I can tell them one thing – they'll always be my friends up here. **99**

Kevin Keegan's *retirement speech after his final game for Newcastle, 1984*

> **"** So look out, Hoddle,
> we've got Waddle
> He takes players on
> – it's one big doddle.
> And new boy Peter,
> runs like a cheetah
> Beardsley's gonna
> be a world-beater! **"**

"Going Up" by Tyneside group **Busker***, 1984*

❝ His enthusiasm has and always will be, incredible and always worth a place in your side. Great players like him write their own scripts. **❞**

Kevin Keegan *on the evergreen Peter Beardsley*

66 The pinnacle of my career has to be wearing the number nine for Newcastle, probably the most famous shirt in British football. I still have one stored under my bed. **99**

Tony Cunningham, *crowd favourite of the 1980s*

" I hated it. The f***ing fans were a bag of shit, the players weren't worth a light. I used to be at the dogs all the time. I bought a couple of greyhounds and thought, "F**k football". **"**

Striker **Billy Whitehurst** on his mixed memories of Newcastle

> **"** If I had known in advance of the two years of heartache I faced when I moved to Newcastle, I would not have taken the job. **"**
>
> **Jim Smith**

" McEwans Best Scotch! "

John Hendrie, *when asked what made him come to Newcastle in 1988*

> The people here love their football and, if you play for Newcastle, they see you as a very special person.

Nolberto Solano

66 Of all the clubs I played for, I still get tingles down the back of my neck thinking about Newcastle. **99**

Mickey Quinn, *former striker*

" Like selling the
family silver... **"**

*Chairman **Gordon McKeag** on giving up
control of the club*

66 My eventual dream is to have 11 Geordies playing for Newcastle United and 11 in the reserves. **99**

Sir John Hall

" Let's kill off once and for all the rumours that Ossie's job is on the line… **"**

Sir John Hall *allays fears that Ardiles will be sacked, 2.4.92*

My heart is broken.

Ossie Ardiles *reacts to his sacking as manager, 5.4.92*

" There's no job in football that I've ever wanted. This is the only job I've ever wanted. **"**

Kevin Keegan *returns as manager, February 1992*

" It wasn't like it said in
the brochure. **"**

Kevin Keegan *walks out on United over broken
promises, March 1992*

" I'd give all this up tonight if it meant that Newcastle, come twenty to five on Saturday, were still in the Second Division. **"**

John Anderson *after his testimonial match, April 1992, with the club deep in relegation trouble*

> **They talk about Newcastle being a sleeping giant but it was more comatose than asleep.**

*Local journalist **Bob Cass**, 1992*

" I picked up an injury and spent quite a lot of time on the bench. One of the supporters knitted me a cushion to sit on, which said, 'Reserved for Brian Kilcline'. **"**

The man also known as **'Killer'** *on home comforts at St James' Park*

" How did we get on? **"**

*Midfielder **Kevin Brock's** question to team-mates on the way back from Birmingham in 1992. He'd ended up in goal and taken a kick in the head for his troubles. United won 3–2*

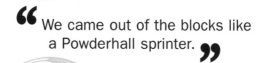

❝ We came out of the blocks like a Powderhall sprinter. **❞**

Kevin Keegan *reflects on the run of 11 league wins at the start of 1992-93*

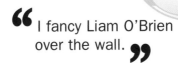

" I fancy Liam O'Brien over the wall. **"**

Lennie Lawrence *predicts United's free-kick winner in the Wear–Tyne derby, 1992*

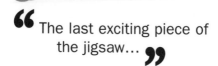

" The last exciting piece of the jigsaw... **"**

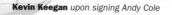

Kevin Keegan *upon signing Andy Cole*

> **If I've got it wrong then there's a bullet with my name on it.**

Kevin Keegan *faces fans the day after selling top-scorer Andy Cole*

66 None of you have any reason to doubt Kevin Keegan or me. We've taken the club from nothingness; we're on course to becoming one of the top three in the UK, the top 10 in Europe. **99**

Sir John Hall, *the following day at the training ground*

> **Mr Keegan, I've never seen such quality football played at such a pace in my life.**

*Royal Antwerp coach, **Urbain Haesaert**, after NUFC's 5-0 win in Belgium, 13.9.94*

" We tried everything to get him. Maybe they offered Sharon Stone. **"**

Tottenham manager **Ossie Ardiles** *on failing to get Philippe Albert, signed by Kevin Keegan*

" With all those replica strips in the stands, coming to Newcastle is like playing in front of 40,000 baying zebras. "

David Pleat, *then Sheffield Wednesday manager*

"I prefer it in Newcastle, knowing all the people want me here. They look me in the eye and say, "I want to play with you."

David Ginola *loses something in the translation*

❝ As soon as I walked into the ground I was greeted by the statue of former striker Malcolm Macdonald. **❞**

David Ginola *gets his numéro neufs confused – he of course meant Jackie Milburn*

> You can't force people to sit down even if they have a seat. They want to sing and, unless you're Val Doonican, you can't do that sitting down.

Kevin Keegan, *1992*

❝ It's like a drug to them, they can't get enough of it. You've got to remember these fans have driven down motorways and watched some really abysmal sides in Newcastle shirts. **❞**

Kevin Keegan *tries to explain 'Toon Army mania'*

" The circus came to town but the lions and tigers didn't turn up. **"**

Kevin Keegan *after losing at Old Trafford in December 1995*

> **66** I've kept really quiet, but I'll tell you something, he went down in my estimation when he said that. But I'll tell ya – you can tell him now if you're watching it – we're still fighting for this title, and he's got to go to Middlesbrough and get something, and… and I tell you honestly, I will love it if we beat them… love it! **99**

Kevin Keegan *feels the heat coming from Alex Ferguson's direction during the Premiership run-in, 1996*

66 It will always rankle with me that we didn't take the title after being so close, but I maintain that Manchester United won it rather than us losing it. 99

Rob Lee *on the lasting disappointment of season 1995–96, when the wrong United won the title*

"Nobody hands you cups
on a plate. **"**

Terry McDermott, *number two to Kevin Keegan*

" We're like the Basques. We are fighting for a nation, the Geordie nation. Football is tribalism and we're the Mohicans. "

Sir John Hall, *1995*

66 The Newcastle Chairman Sir John Hall went on the record to claim that Les Ferdinand would be leaving Newcastle "over my dead body" – I wonder if he is still alive. 99

Les Ferdinand

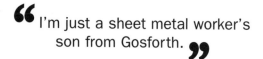

66 I'm just a sheet metal worker's son from Gosforth. **99**

Alan Shearer, *local hero, 1996*

" I wanted to wear that number nine shirt and nothing was going to derail me from getting it. **"**

Alan Shearer

" The two seasons we played together at Newcastle were like Heaven. **"**

'Sir' Les Ferdinand *on his devastating partnership with Alan Shearer*

66 To call football religion is too much. But there's no doubt that, in places like Newcastle, when they've got a good team and are playing well, then the spirits of the people are lifted. **99**

Cardinal Basil Hume *on football's place in the scheme of things*

I don't f**king believe it!

Malcolm Allison's *live commentary on Century Radio, as Les Ferdinand scores Newcastle's winner against Middlesbrough, 1996*

" He's not a player you can tell to do this or do that, you just have to let him get on with it. **"**

Kevin Keegan *after Tino Asprilla's debut, February 1996*

66 When he first came he wanted to get a fishing boat so they took him to Tynemouth the first weekend he was here. He took one look at the North Sea and said, "F**k that!" 99

Tino Asprilla's interpreter **Nick Emerson**

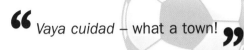

" *Vaya cuidad – what a town!* **"**

Tino Asprilla *after his first visit to Newcastle's famous Bigg Market*

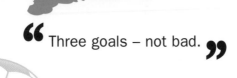

66 Three goals – not bad. **99**

Tino Asprilla's *appraisal of his stunning hat-trick against Barcelona, 1997*

" He's just handed in a written transfer request. The handwriting was beautiful. **"**

Kenny Dalglish *on David Ginola*

66 At Newcastle I was older than the manager, older than the assistant manager, older than the physio and the club doctor – which must be some sort of record. 99

Stuart Pearce *recounts life as captain of Newcastle's Dad's Army*

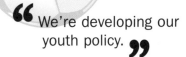

66 We're developing our youth policy. **99**

Kenny Dalglish *after Ian Rush joined fellow veteran John Barnes in Toon*

❝ You know what Newcastle are like. You never know what's going to happen. **❞**

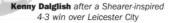

Kenny Dalglish *after a Shearer-inspired 4-3 win over Leicester City*

❝ I've been out of short trousers for a long time now and I'm not going to say this is the worst day of my life. **❞**

Kenny Dalglish *after being sacked, August 1998*

"Is Kenny Dalglish a big girl's blouse?"

Jeremy Paxman *provocatively opens up a* Newsnight *debate on football managers*

" We'll play you anywhere –
Hackney Marshes – we're
not frightened. **"**

Kenny Dalglish *in a phone call to
Stevenage Borough FC after a rumpus over
Broadhall Way's fitness to host an FA Cup tie*

> **The only Irishman who didn't know where Dublin was.**

Unnamed reporter on **Radio 5 Live** *after Shay Given failed to spot Coventry's No.9 lurking when he put the ball down in his own area. Dublin scored*

66 I was very happy, not angry, when I scored and I always celebrate in an unusual way. I threw it to a good fan and I would have got another from the bench. I knew what I was doing. Everyone congratulated me in the dressing room. **99**

Temuri Ketsbaia *on his manic hoarding-abusing goal celebration versus Bolton, 1998*

66 You never sell the fur of a bear before you shoot it. I have brought my cannon with me. **99**

*A cryptic **Ruud Gullit** on his bid to sign Ibrahim Ba*

❝ I know the players I want. It is like I have them in the fridge waiting to come out. **❞**

Ruud Gullit *gives his current squad the cold shoulder*

> **When I arrived, the fans called me a thieving Spaniard and a bloody gypsy who was robbing the club's cash.**

Marcelino, *who is unlikely to return to the North-East on holiday*

66 I couldn't tell you what the atmosphere is like there now, I don't understand half the players because they are foreign. Now I'm at Villa, I'm the one with the funny accent. **99**

*A rueful **Steve Watson** tries to sum up his days under the Gullit regime*

❝ I'll be bringing the pigeons up to Newcastle with me, but I'll have to bring them up in the car. They're not good enough to find their own way here yet! **❞**

Bird-fancier **Duncan Ferguson** *at his first Newcastle press conference*

66 It was f****n' magic! When big Dunc Ferguson scored, I bloody exploded oot me seat, and so did Keegan! 99

*AC/DC Singer **Bryan Johnson** recalls a visit to see his beloved black and whites*

" The added benefits of the new kit will give Newcastle an edge on the field of play and the white socks will give us an advantage over the opposition. "

Ruud Gullit's *fashion forecasts prove to be a tad optimistic as United flop under his leadership*

" I don't care if they ban me or fine me. Fine me what you like – I will pay it and I will still be right. I know I am right. Never in all my career have I seen a referee influence a game like that. He destroyed it, and I blame him for us losing the game. I can't blame it on myself, my team or Aston Villa. It was the referee and nothing else. **"**

*An incandescent **Ruud Gullit** reacts to Alan Shearer's red card, 1999*

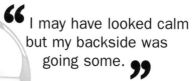

66 I may have looked calm but my backside was going some. **99**

Alan Shearer *after his successful penalty in the*
FA Cup semi-final v Spurs, 11.3.99

66 Not a team sheet but a
suicide note. **99**

Journalist **Tim Rich's** *comment after Ruud Gullit
omits Alan Shearer from his team to face
Sunderland, 1999*

> ❝ Next morning I decided to have it out with the manager. Dunc (Duncan Ferguson) had beaten me to it and the door to the manager's office was already off its hinges when I got to the training ground. ❞

Alan Shearer *remembering a rare occasion when Duncan Ferguson used his pace to good effect.*

66 I haven't resigned; my mother hasn't got chicken pox; I haven't bought a house; I haven't been offered a job with the national team; I haven't been offered a job in America; I'm still here; my wife is okay; my daughter is okay; the groundsman is okay; everybody at Newcastle is okay. 99

Ruud Gullit, *21.8.99, a week before his resignation*

66 When I came, people asked me if I knew how big the job was. Now I know what they meant. 99

Gullit *resigns, 28.8.99*

112

66 There was no hiding the fact that me and Ruud didn't see eye to eye, but I was as surprised as anyone when I heard the news. I always said no individual is bigger than any football club. **99**

Alan Shearer's *reaction to Gullit's departure three days after losing the Tyne-Wear derby*

" If you asked what would be my one wish, it would be to go back to England and, in one mad, great year, take over one club and win the championship. And I'd feel, well, I'd done it. **"**

*Then manager of Porto, **Bobby Robson** hints at a return to the old country*

" A great appointment. He obviously loves the club, which is really important. I'm not saying Kenny Dalglish and Ruud Gullit didn't love the club, but Bobby knows the place, because it's in his heart – and I think that is a massive advantage. **"**

Kevin Keegan *on Bobby Robson's appointment*

> **❝** It's lovely that he's in charge of his hometown club and that pride just oozes out of him. **❞**

Brian Clough *gets sentimental about Bobby Robson*

" We've got to batten down the hatches, plug a few leaks and get the ship sailing again. **"**

Robson *takes over HMS Newcastle United*

" He saved my career in a way, because I was down in the dumps when he came to Newcastle – he got me back to playing the way that I know I can. **"**

Alan Shearer *on Bobby Robson*

" Happy Birthday – any chance
of a rise? "

*Message from **Alan Shearer** in a card marking*
Sir Bobby Robson's 70th birthday

The manager said at half time if I got six he might give me a Mars bar. I'll have to go out and buy my own now, won't I?

Alan Shearer *on 'only scoring five' against Sheffield Wednesday in an 8–0 success.*

66 The Commission accepted that the incident was initially caused by Neil Lennon pulling at the shirt of Alan Shearer turning round and trapping his leg. It further accepted that the alleged incident of Alan Shearer swinging out with his left leg was a genuine attempt to free himself. **99**

FA Commission report *clearing Alan Shearer of assaulting Leicester City's Neil Lennon, 2000*

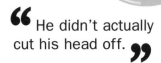

" He didn't actually cut his head off. **"**

Fergie *responds to Roy Keane's dismissal after a clash with Alan Shearer, 15.9.01*

" He's grinning. "You prick". He gestures dismissively. The red card comes out. Shearer's right. I am a prick. **"**

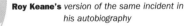

Roy Keane's *version of the same incident in his autobiography*

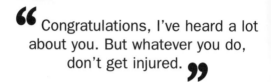

❝ Congratulations, I've heard a lot about you. But whatever you do, don't get injured. **❞**

*New United boss **Bobby Robson** meets Kieron Dyer – on the pitch at Wembley before England v Luxembourg, 1999*

" He's got this terrific little engine, I don't know where he gets his petrol from – I could do with some of that. "

Bobby Robson *on Kieron Dyer*

❝ I'm looking for a goalkeeper with three legs. ❞

Bobby Robson *after Shay Given is nutmegged twice by Marcus Bent of Ipswich Town*

" Sad and miserable, but very effective. **"**

Bobby Robson *on Wimbledon after they'd beaten Newcastle 2–0*

❝ Bellamy came on at Liverpool and did well, but everyone thinks that he's the saviour, that he's Jesus Christ. He's not Jesus Christ. **❞**

Bobby Robson *debunks an unlikely myth*

66 They can't be monks – we don't want them to be monks; we want them to be football players because a monk doesn't play football at this level. **99**

Bobby Robson *on the habits of his playing staff*

" If we invite any player up to the quayside to see the girls and then up to our magnificent stadium, we will be able to persuade any player to sign. "

Bobby Robson *on the myriad attractions of Tyneside*

66 We mustn't be despondent.
We don't have to play them every
week – although we do play them
next week as it happens. **99**

Bobby Robson *after a 2–0 league defeat to Arsenal who
United face a week later in the FA Cup*

66 Newcastle had not won in 29 games and two plus nine is 11. While they were scoring the winning goals, I was running round the outside of the ground 11 times to lift the hoodoo. I arrived late and had no ticket. But the moment I got out of the car and touched the Highbury stadium, Ray Parlour was sent off. **99**

Uri Geller *takes all the credit for ending Newcastle's thirty-game winless run in London, December 2001*

❝ Robson the man I don't really know. I just know Robson the manager. **❞**

*Newcastle chairman, **Freddy Shepherd**, explains his relationship with Bobby Robson*

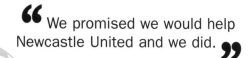

“ We promised we would help Newcastle United and we did. **”**

Roberto Bettega, *Juventus vice-president, after Juve's victory in Kiev, which helps put United into the second round of the Champions League, 2002*

66 I'm pretty ecstatic – but
I'm pretty numb as well,
so I'm a bit of both. **99**

Bobby Robson *after victory at Feyenoord gives
Newcastle a chance of qualification for the
Champions League second round, 2002*

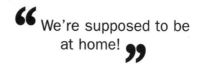

We're supposed to be at home!

Newcastle fans *singing in Barcelona, 11.12.02,*
after torrential rain saw their game postponed for
24 hours

" We've enjoyed the ride, we've paid the money, got the ride, got off the tramcar – let's go again. We can do better. **"**

Bobby Robson *after the Barcelona home defeat ended the Champions League adventure, 2003*

" That's the way I am and I always will be. After all, I kick Laurent Robert in training – and he's one of our players. **"**

Andrew Griffin *on his no-nonsense philosophy*

" Carl Cort. "

Shola Ameobi, *when asked what*
Bobby Robson called him

66 I can't sit there laughing, can I? Is that what you want? Ha ha ha – like that? Oh, penalty, ha ha. Oh, it's saved. Ha ha. No, it's gone in. Ha ha. What do you expect me to look like? **99**

Bobby Robson's *reply to a journalist querying his downcast expression, 2003*

66 We're in a dog fight, and the fight in the dog will get us out of trouble. We are solid behind each other, and through being solid we will get out of trouble and, if that fails, then we will be in trouble, but that's not the situation here. We'll all get in the same rowing boat, and we'll all pick up an oar and we'll row the boat. **99**

Bobby Robson *in Churchillian mode, 2003*

❝ This is a fantastic football club with great spirit and a public that live, breathe and die for everything that goes on here. **❞**

*A defiant **Bobby Robson** after United's loss to Partizan Belgrade, 2003*

66 I've only got two words for how we played out there tonight – not good enough. **99**

Bobby Robson

"There is no hesitation by the club in recording its sincere appreciation for the way in which Sir Bobby has handled team affairs during that five-year spell which has seen a significant turnaround in the club's fortunes."

Newcastle statement, *August 2004*

" I was about to enter a period of life that I can only really describe as a kind of bereavement. **"**

Sir Bobby Robson *on being sacked in August 2004*

66 I don't need to be told by anyone that Newcastle are one of the best supported clubs around. Everything is geared to be successful, and I hope I can bring sucess. **99**

Graeme Souness, *takes over at Newcastle, September 2004*

" Sou Long. **"**

The Sun's headline when Souness was sacked,
February 2006

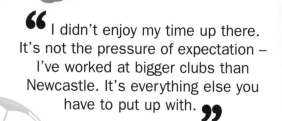

" I didn't enjoy my time up there. It's not the pressure of expectation – I've worked at bigger clubs than Newcastle. It's everything else you have to put up with. **"**

Graeme Souness

66 I could sign a bad player every day between now and 31 January. There are plenty out there. **99**

A frustrated **Glenn Roeder**, *January 2007 transfer window*

> **Alan Shearer is boring – we call him Mary Poppins.**

*A small sample of what **Freddy Shepherd and John Hall** wanted to have banned*

66 If someone wants to keep something confidential, talking about it in a Spanish brothel is not the way to do it. **99**

Justice Lindsay *refuses to grant an injuncion against the* News of the World *newspaper on behalf of Freddy Shepherd and Douglas Hall*

> "I wanted to score goals at St James' Park. I've lived my dream and I realise how lucky I've been to have done that."

*Injury forces **Alan Shearer** to retire early, April 2006*

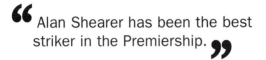

66 Alan Shearer has been the best striker in the Premiership. **99**

Alan Hansen

“ I'm a very happy man tonight. I know what Jackie means and meant to the people. I can now sleep easy that the pressure has gone. **”**

Alan Shearer grabs his 201st United goal in February 2006, breaking Jackie Milburn's Newcastle goalscoring record

" It's been everything I hoped for and more playing for Newcastle. The only – and it's a big only – thing that's missing is the silverware. Everything else has been fantastic. "

Alan Shearer

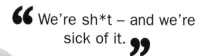

We're sh*t – and we're sick of it.

Newcastle fans *at Wigan, December 2007*

" I'm not suited to Bolton or Blackburn, I would be more suited to Internazionale or Real Madrid. It wouldn't be a problem to me to go and manage those clubs because I would win the Double or the league every time. **"**

Sam Allardyce, *three months before Blackburn's owners agreed – and sacked him*

❝ He's got cash to invest. With his contacts abroad, he'll make Newcastle well known. We'll win things under him and we'll also get a global perspective. He's a very nice fellow. **❞**

Sir John Hall *on Mike Ashley*

“ I would say Newcastle are the most difficult club to manage in the game, gobbling up managers and spitting them out again with hardly a pause. If they regarded their managers as something more than ships that pass in the night they might achieve the stability and consistency that is the basis of success at any club. **”**

Sir Alex Ferguson *defines Geordie RSI*

" Mike's a guy that likes to talk to the fans, the everyday person, before the game. I had trouble getting him out of the pub to get him there for kick-off. **"**

Derek Llambias *on owner Mike Ashley*

> **"** Mike was offered a drink which he thought was non-alcoholic so he took it in good faith. **"**

Club statement *after the Newcastle owner is caught on camera downing a pint at Arsenal's Emirates Stadium.*

66 When they've worked all week, for them the match is a bit like people down south going to the theatre. They want to see something that's worth seeing. Provided it's a really good show, even if it doesn't work out quite the way they wanted, they'll go home thinking, "That was good". 99

Never say never – **Kevin Keegan** *returns to Tyneside, January 2008*

" We're a million miles away from challenging for the league, but if my owner backs me, and I have no proof of that but no doubt he will, we want to try to finish fifth and top of the other mini-league. I get on great with the owner because I never talk to him. **"**

Kevin Keegan, *May 2008 – four games before he left United once again*

"Cockney Mafia Out!"

Newcastle fans *unfurl a banner in mid-match following the departure of Kevin Keegan*

" I have the interests of Newcastle United at heart. I have listened to you. You want me out. That is what I am now trying to do but it won't happen overnight and it may not happen at all if a buyer does not come in. You don't need to demonstrate against me again because I have got the message. **"**

*Part of **Mike Ashley's** "I'm off" 1,644-word statement, September 2008*

" It cannot be tolerated, it needs to be kicked out of the game. **"**

*Hull City boss **Phil Brown** on the tackle that left Tigers player Craig Fagan with a broken leg*

❝ As we come to the end of the year, I hope ... that you all go home smiling today after a win against Liverpool to end 2008 on a high ... and if, like me, you like a gamble now and again then what price a flutter on us reaching that top six? **❞**

Mike Ashley's *2009 message to supporters: United lost 1–5 and were relegated*

> **"** We declare that Kevin Keegan was constructively dismissed by Newcastle United Football Club Limited for which Newcastle United Football Club Limited must pay to Kevin Keegan damages in the sum of £2 million plus interest to be assessed if not agreed. **"**

Judgement in the Kevin Keegan v NUFC court case

> **"**The system imposed at Newcastle just did not work and it is as simple as that. **"**

Former Executive Director (football)
Dennis Wise *states the obvious*

" The board of Newcastle United can today confirm that the club is for sale at the price of £100 million. Interested parties should contact Newcastle United at admin@nufc.co.uk. **"**

A new low

" Success, really, will heal the wounds, and time, a combination of both. We are patient people and I think the fans will come around eventually. I have no idea what length of time that will be – I may be a very old man before it's done – but I think the fans will see in the future that we do care. **"**

Derek Llambias *remains in defiant mood*

66 I will pick two local papers and speak to them and the rest can f*ck off. I ain't coming up here to have the p*ss taken out of me. I have a million pages of crap that has been written about me. **99**

Joe Kinnear's *expletive-ridden first press conference*

66 You can see why a lot of big names out there didn't have the arsehole to take this job. You can see why so many people bottled it. **99**

More purple prose from **Joe Kinnear**

66 Shay [Given] pulled out with a knee injury as did Insomnia ... Insomnia ... er, Charlie. **99**

Joe Kinnear *tries in vain to pronounce N'Zogbia, who wasn't impressed*

" Everyone at Newcastle United is absolutely delighted that Alan has taken on this challenge. Already there is a buzz around the club and the city. The news has given everyone a massive boost. **"**

Derek Llambias *greets Alan Shearer as manager –*
on April Fools' Day

> **"** He is a very popular choice and it's a little bit of mental doping for the whole Newcastle area because it will give them belief and hope again. **"**

Arsene Wenger *praises the appointment of Wor Al*

" I wasn't good enough, Mike Ashley wasn't good enough and Chris Hughton, Joe Kinnear and Kevin Keegan before that weren't good enough. But it's what is in the dressing-room that has got us relegated. It has been a problem all season. **"**

Alan Shearer *reacts to Newcastle's Premier League relegation*

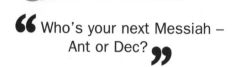

" Who's your next Messiah –
Ant or Dec? **"**

Aston Villa fan *banner, May 2009*

" Newcastle is a nice city to live in. I was surprised because I had heard many legends about England. About the weather, the food and the time everything closes. But I loved it. **"**

*Misfit striker **Xisco** loves the Toon – £50K a week might also help ...*

> **"** The Athlete. The Ambassador. The Icon … Michael will be shortly out of contract and may consider a challenge away from St James' Park. **"**

*Part of the nausea-inducing 32 page brochure circulated by **Michael Owen** following relegation*

66 Prefer playing less often in a top team than every game in a poor team. Been there and didn't enjoy it. **99**

Michael Owen *continues to make new friends on Tyneside*

66 Chris [Hughton] is our manager and will remain our manager and it is our intention to re-negotiate his contract at the end of the year. **99**

Club statement *on 27.10.10*

66 Newcastle United have today parted company with Chris Hughton … the board now feels that an individual with more managerial experience is needed to take the club forward. **99**

Club statement *on 6.12.10*

" This is a club in my heart, it grew that way. It is an amazing city – a tight place where everyone adores the club. It is a one-city club and it is almost unique in the way everyone wears the shirts. You come to the ground and see women, kids, the whole family with their shirts on. "

Nicky Butt *pays tribute to the Toon Army following his retirement*

66 Ultimately the fans don't support me, they support the shirt. 99

Alan Pardew *after his first game as Newcastle manager, December 2010*

66 He is not for sale. I am going to say it for one last time, he is not for sale. **99**

Alan Pardew's *infamous Andy Carroll soundbite*

" I saw an interview where Alan Pardew said he hoped to get some of that £35 million. I thought: "Alan, you ain't going to get any of that." **"**

Kevin Keegan *twists the knife over the destination of the Andy Carroll transfer fee*

> **"** If the Arsenal players don't like being tackled, they should go and play basketball or netball or one of the other games. **"**

Joey Barton *following "that" 4-4 draw with Arsenal*

66 I don't know whether people are going to buy me a drink or throw them at me – that's the sort of week it's been. **99**

Alan Pardew *prepares for a night on the Toon after the 4–4 draw*

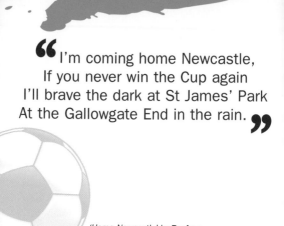

> **❝** I'm coming home Newcastle,
> If you never win the Cup again
> I'll brave the dark at St James' Park
> At the Gallowgate End in the rain. **❞**

'Home Newcastle' by **Busker**

❝ I've known him since he was 6ft 3ins! **❞**

*Magpies goalkeeper **Steve Harper** on Andy Carroll*

“ What is a club in any case? Not the buildings or the directors or the people who are paid to represent it. It's not the television contracts, get-out clauses, marketing departments or executive boxes. It's the noise, the passion, the feeling of belonging, the pride in your city. It's a small boy clambering up stadium steps for the very first time, gripping his father's hand, gawping at that hallowed stretch of turf beneath him and, without being able to do a thing about it, falling in love. **”**

Final word to the late, great **Sir Bobby Robson**